Art Nouveau Posters
Make Your Own Art Masterpiece

Publisher and Creative Director: Nick Wells
Art Director: Mike Spender
Editorial: Gillian Whitaker
Illustrator: David Jones
Colours: Federica Ciaravella

FLAME TREE PUBLISHING
6 Melbray Mews
Fulham, London SW6 3NS
United Kingdom

www.flametreepublishing.com

First published 2019

19 21 23 22 20
1 3 5 7 9 10 8 6 4 2

A CIP record for this book is available from the British Library upon request.

ISBN 978-1-78755-290-6

Printed in China

Art Nouveau Posters
Make Your Own Art Masterpiece

Illustrated by David Jones

Selected by Daisy Seal

FLAME TREE
PUBLISHING

Here are some of the hues used in this book. Use these
as a starting point for your own art masterpieces.

Art Nouveau Posters

The era of the Art Nouveau poster at the turn of the twentieth century was one of optimism and excitement: it was a time of new technologies and social upheaval, with vibrant theatres, music halls and other places of leisure providing entertainment for everyone rather than just the social elite. Cities such as Paris and Vienna became the centres for this new cultural phenomenon, and the mass-produced posters acted as an expression of the epoch's joie de vivre and confidence.

Even though most of the posters made at the end of the century were produced using lithography, they channel the essence of early nineteenth century Japanese woodblock prints in their use of flat blocks of colour and simplified forms. This allowed them to promote idealized visions for the products they advertised: instead of depicting realism, artists incorporated a recognizable style that presented consumer items as part of a glamorous lifestyle. For the first time typography and design were given equal weight to the content advertised, and the poster became an art form in its own right. This collection of designs celebrates the likes of Jules Chéret (1836–1932), Henri de Toulouse-Lautrec (1864–1901), Théophile-Alexandre Steinlen (1859–1923) and Alphonse Mucha (1860–1939), and the masterful ways they communicated the spirit of the age through their art posters.

∽

Illustration based on advertising poster for

Manufacture Royale de Corsets, 1897

by Henri Privat-Livemont (1861–1936)

Illustration based on advertising poster for

Divan Japonais, 1892

by Henri de Toulouse-Lautrec (1864–1901)

Illustration based on advertising poster for

The Musical Comedy 'A Gaiety Girl', c. 1893–95

by Dudley Hardy (1867–1922)

Illustration based on advertising poster for

Le Chat Noir Cabaret, 1896

by Théophile-Alexandre Steinlen (1859–1923)

Illustration based on advertising poster for

Monaco – Monte Carlo, 1897

by Alphonse Mucha (1860–1939)

Illustration based on advertising poster for

Peugeot Bicycles, c. 1905–10

by Walter Thor (1870–1929)

Illustration based on advertising poster for

Harper's March, 1895

by Edward Penfield (1866–1925)

HARPER'S

HARPER'S MAGAZINE

MARCH

Illustration based on advertising poster for

Chocolat Menier, 1893

by Firmin Bouisset (1859–1925)

Illustration based on advertising poster for

The Tissue Paper 'Abadie', 1898

by Henri Gray (1858–1924)

Illustration based on advertising poster for

Katabexine Effervescent Tablets, 1898

by Leonetto Cappiello (1875–1942)

Illustration based on advertising poster for

The Illustrated Pall Mall Budget, 1896

by Maurice Greiffenhagen (1862–1931)

Illustration based on advertising poster for

Lance Parfum 'Rodo', 1896

by Alphonse Mucha (1860–1939)

Illustration based on advertising poster for

The Sun Newspaper, 1895

by Louis John Rhead (1857–1926)

Illustration based on advertising poster for

The Café-Concert 'Alcazar d'Été', 1890

by Jules Chéret (1836–1932)

Illustration based on advertising poster for

Clinique Chéron, 1905

by Théophile-Alexandre Steinlen (1859–1923)

Illustration based on advertising poster for

A Grasset Exhibition at the Salon des Cent, 1894

by Eugène Grasset (1841–1917)

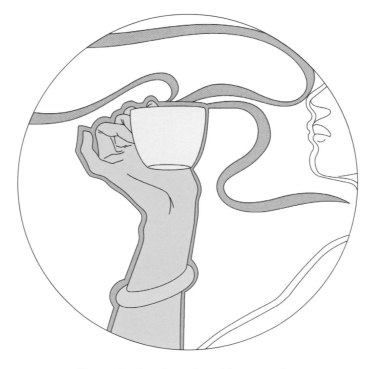

Illustration based on advertising poster for

Rajah Tea, 1897

by Henri Meunier (1873–1922)

Illustration based on advertising poster for

Lefèvre-Utile Gaufrettes Vanille, 1897

by Alphonse Mucha (1860–1939)

Illustration based on advertising poster for

L'Ermitage, 1897

by Paul Berthon (1872–1909)

Illustration based on advertising poster for

**The Fifth Annual Exhibition of the Cercle
Artistique de Schaerbeek, Galerie Manteau, 1897**

by Henri Privat-Livemont (1861–1936)

Illustration based on advertising poster for

Germaine Gallois in the 'Scala' Revue, 1901

by Maurice Biais (1875–1926)

Illustration based on advertising poster for

Women Suffrage, c. 1905

by Evelyn Rumsey Cary (1855–1924)

Illustration based on advertising poster for

The Morning Journal, 1895

by Louis John Rhead (1857–1926)

Illustration based on advertising poster for

Quinquina Dubonnet, 1895

by Jules Chéret (1836–1932)

Illustration based on advertising poster for

Robette Absinthe, 1896

by Henri Privat-Livemont (1861–1936)

Illustration based on advertising poster for

Joan of Arc Costumes, 1896

by Georges de Feure (1868–1943)

Illustration based on advertising poster for

Liane de Pougy at the Folies Bergère, *c.* 1890

by Paul Berthon (1872–1909)

Illustration based on advertising poster for

The Printer Charles Verneau, titled 'La Rue', 1896

by Théophile-Alexandre Steinlen (1859–1923)

Illustration based on advertising poster for

Sarah Bernhardt as Gismonda at the Théâtre de la Renaissance, 1894

by Alphonse Mucha (1860–1939)

Illustration based on advertising poster for

Crescent Cycles, 1899

by Frederick Winthrop Ramsdell (1865–1915)

Illustration based on advertising poster for

The Newspaper 'Jugend', 1896

by Ludwig von Zumbusch (1861–1927)

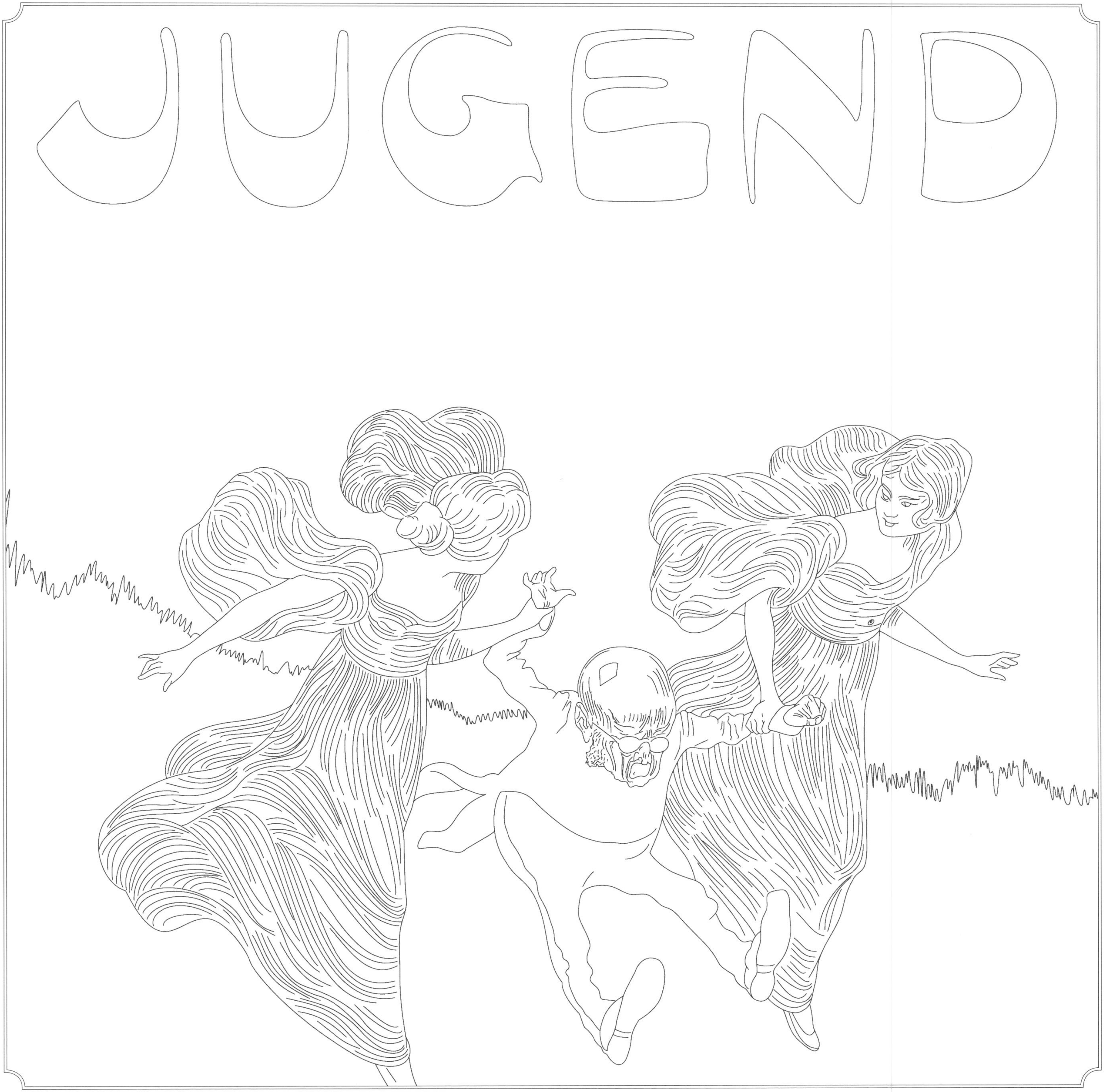
JUGEND

Illustration based on advertising poster for

Lithographies Originales, 1896

by Georges de Feure (1868–1943)

Illustration based on advertising poster for

Concerts Ysaÿe, Salle du Cirque Royal, 1895–96

by Henri Meunier (1873–1922)

Illustration based on advertising poster for

Chocolat Idéal, 1897

by Alphonse Mucha (1860–1939)

Illustration based on advertising poster for

Cachou Lajaunie, *c.* 1922

by Leonetto Cappiello (1875–1942)

Illustration based on advertising poster for

Phénix Beer, *c.* 1899

by Adolf Hohenstein (1854–1928)

Illustration based on advertising poster for

The Scottish Musical Review, 1896

by Charles Rennie Mackintosh (1868–1928)

Illustration based on advertising poster for

Cycles Perfecta, 1902

by Alphonse Mucha (1860–1939)

Illustration based on advertising poster for

The Quartier Latin: A Magazine Devoted to The Arts, *c.* 1898–99

by Louis John Rhead (1857–1926)

Illustration based on advertising poster for

Amatller Chocolates, 1903

Illustration based on advertising poster for

The Matterhorn, Zermatt, 1908

by Emil Cardinaux (1877–1936)

Illustration based on advertising poster for

Aristide Bruant at the Ambassadeurs, 1892

by Henri de Toulouse-Lautrec (1864–1901)

Illustration based on advertising poster for

Moët & Chandon Champagne 'White Star', 1899

by Alphonse Mucha (1860–1939)

Illustration based on advertising poster for

Sterilized Milk from La Vingeanne, 1894

by Théophile-Alexandre Steinlen (1859–1923)

Illustration based on advertising poster for

L. Marquet Ink: 'The Best of All Inks', 1892

by Franz Grassel (1861–*c.* 1921)

For further illustrated books on a wide range of

art subjects, in various formats, please look at our website:

www.flametreepublishing.com